DEDICATED TO MY SWEET SONS WHO GIVE ME STRENGTH & INSPIRATION EVERY DAY.

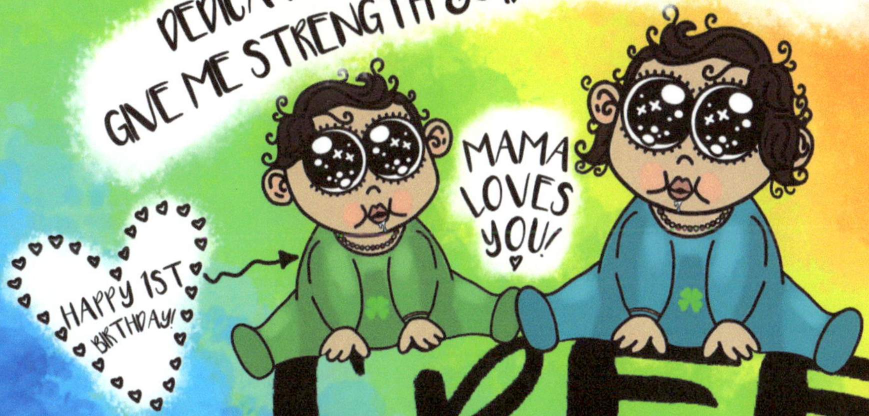

FREE OR FORCE?

www.LuLuLotus.ca

Some people see what they want to see.

It might
look like fun

BUT

It doesn't need
to be done!

Killer whales don't want to be stuck in tanks

They want to be free!
BORIS
GEORGE
MARCO
ROZINA

CHARLOTTE
CHASE
Dolphins don't want to take pictures with you

JADE
PINKY
SPARKLES
They want to be free!
FLOWER
SONIC

Tigers don't want to jump through fire at the circus
IAN

They want to be free!
CELESTE
XANDER
LILY

Elephants don't want to give you rides
$15 ELEPHANT RIDES
DAISY

They want to be free!
SARAH
ELLIE
BELLA

Camels don't want to race

They want to be free!
- EMMA
ILAM
EOIN

Lions don't want to live in the zoo
LOOMIS

They want
to be free!
LITTLE LULU
LEO
STAR
SPARKLE
ORION

Horses don't want to pull your carriage

They want to be free!
POGO
MARIGOLD

Fish don't want to be caught
NEMO
JASMINE
CHARLEE
RYLEE
GOLDFISH

They want to be free!
ZOFIA
ELENA
MATILDA
VANESSA
DAP DAP

Chimpanzees
don't want
to be
on TV

KIWI
CLEMINTINE
JAMIE
DAISY
They want to be free!

parrots don't want to live in cages

They want to be free!

Calves don't want to
be in the rodeo
CHOCOLATE

They want to be free!
SWEET PEA
SUNSHINE

Foxes don't want to be trapped by hunters
ROXY

They want to
be free!

KADENCE
TORA
ALEX
DALLAS

I hope this book
has helped you see
that animals are
happier when
they are
FREE!

COLOURING
PAGE

THANK YOU!

YOUR CREATIVE CHARACTER NAMES WERE GREAT!

Nathan Bonder
Maya Bonder
Nora Ahmad
Sara Ahmad
Kali Burnett
Billy Pasidis
Ilam Flores
Emma Flores
Eoin Flores
Jayden Closs
Jacob Closs
Maliyah Closs-Walton
Xavier D'Andrea
Mikaela D'Andrea
Vania Galicia
Genesis Galicia
Landon Leaming
Rilee-Paige Leaming
Sapphire Leaming
Peyton Korek
Kendyl Michelle Adair
Kenya Jade

Leo Lyth Hassan
Keegan Smith
Kadence King
Dallas King
Alex King
Tora King
Jayden OFlaherty
Masyn Zita
Deegan Zita
Grace Sutherland
Isabelle Turner
Blaine Witty
Ethan B.
Emilia B.
Alexis Jordan
Aleigha Jordan
Easton Wilson
Chloe Jensen
Zofia Gralewska Begley
Elena Gralewska Begley
Matilda Gralewska Begley
Prince David S.
Vanessa Gracey

Zachary Barrett-Cepero
Nicholas Barrett
Noëlla Martina
Liam Accoumeh
Lilianna Accoumeh
Aidan Baldwin
Graham Jackson
Tandra Drew
Emma Lasky
Nicholas Lasky
Zadie Reed
Razzek Reed
Shanaya Kumar
Yusef Elmes
Aliyah Riley Cordeiro
Jade Spiegelberg
Maya Ambro
Kayleigh Blake
Jasmine Shonias
Alex Shonias
Rylee McPhee
Ian Felix
Alayna Grace